MOTHER OF NATIONS

Poems

MOTHER OF NATIONS

Poems

Dawn Karima

First U.S. edition 2019

Editor and Publisher: Laura LeHew

Proofreaders: Nancy Carol Moody
                       Keli Osborn

Cover Art: Born for Bear Clan People and born to the Mud
                       People, Keith Jim is Diné from the Navajo tribe.
                       He has spent most of his life drawing. His comic
                       book, *The Heros,* which was recently released,
                       represents his dream come true. He draws to
                       bring awareness to Native American issues and
                       can be reached at Monsterslayersart@gmail.com
                       and KeithjimArts on Facebook.

                       "Mother of Nations" © Keith Jim

Uttered Chaos
PO Box 50638
Eugene, OR 97405
www.utteredchaos.org

ISBN: 978-0-9998334-3-8

This book is for my Babies, who make me a Mother of Nations. I love you forever and all the days.

CONTENTS

MOTHER OF NATIONS

Tracks lead straight to the heart of the matter,

Songs of the stars made flesh and bone.

Lamentation lost in the whirlwind,

Peace since wherever you are is home.

A lullaby spun from the Sun and Moon crying,

Sighing, scorching Earth as a soulful pyre,

Turning tides meant to inspire desire,

We make a map of the world in the flames of

our fire.

QUEEN OF LOVE

I decolonize myself by laughing.
My soft tongue will break your bones,
Bite apples of gold from settings of silver.
Just 30 pieces will ransom our lives.

Where 40 acres and a mule rule,
My laughter is a salve,
That halves the steps of righteous men,
Ordered, bordered by round dance songs,
Wrongs, righted and set upright
As my giggling heals.

Hear me as you break your treaties
Fear my happy bliss of hope,
My smile is, for a little space,
Grace,
And my joy is a medicine song.

FRUIT OF THE WOMB

Each Stomp,
Each step
Reveals
The precious fruit of the sun,
Honors
The precious things of the moon,
Secretly brought
In thoughts.
Our sleep flees
Until we call on One who will answer,
Rise and tie shakers of earth and turtle heartbeats,
Shake shells under songs.
Each Stomp,
Each step
Reveals
Creator sitting on the circle of the world.
We call Him with tongues of fire.
When He answers,
The fruit of the womb is ours.

ECHOTA TRIBAL PSALM

Songs echo in the air
Memories in mountains,
Told again in thunder,
In drumbeats,
And dance.

Dancers are our poetry.
Warriors are our art.
We hold our history,
In hawk and macaw feathers.

The Trail of Tears wounded us in the house of our friends,
Echota faces tilted toward the whirlwind,
Waiting for Spirit to do us justice,
Come, Creator, hear and help.

We call You, Most Ancient of Drums.

STAR SONGS

We come with offerings of sourwood honey.
We build your altar with stones from our mountains.
We regret that we have no gold.
The conquistadors stole it and left us smallpox.
The silver we offer is commodity cans, papered with labels.
Our frankincense is the smell of cedar, the odor of honeysuckle, wet
after rain.
We have no myrrh.
Genocide took it.
Help us, Creator.
We hear you as the stars sing.

Mvskoke Milk and Honey

Birdie Marvelous Recovering

I.   Fakke (Earth)

I surprise everyone and no one when I fall to Earth.

The slick, red bottoms of my glittering stiletto heels slide across the grass outside the concert hall. My crimson fingernails claw into the ground. I am cupping a handful of dirt in my palm when the paramedics place me in the ambulance that will carry me to a hospital that the paparazzi surround. My designer lace evening gown is streaked with soil. Flashes flicker like tiny meteors, carrying gossip and stardom into every place where I am known.

I surprise myself when I return to the reservation.

"You need to file this one under 'damn shame,'" my agent sneers when I tell him I am going back to Creek Nation. "All that insurance and all those doctors and all they can come up with is 'exhaustion.' You need to get UN-exhausted already ... all those pictures of you collapsing at the Grammys in the tabloids ... you're white-hot right about now."

"White-hot. That's funny." Most everything in the hospital seems funny. Must be all the medicine. Or the oxygen is bubbling in my head. "I'm Native American, Ira," I reply. "Creek. If I'm hot, I'm RED-hot."

My agent interrupts my laughter. "Whatever. Hot doesn't last. Neither does February. Get yourself together and get back in the game."

I stare at the IV in my arm for a while after he hangs up. When I gaze out of the ICU window, the crest of the moon is upside down.

II.   HUTE (HOME)

"What you need is an Indian Doctor," Granny Estomahe declares. My *puse* stands in the doorway of her tiny house, holding open the screened door with one hand and beckoning me in with the other. My *puca,* Granddaddy Estomahe, baked each earthen brick and laid it into the order of every wall in their shotgun house. When Granny Estomahe agreed to marry him, he drew her name in the wet cement of the front steps. *Fuslane Estomahe*, Yellowbird Marvelous, greets me now. She shows no surprise that I am here.

"I sent your Uncle and Auntie for The Indian Doctor," Granny Estomahe pronounces. "Take off them sunglasses and let me look at you." She studies me. Then she wets the edge of her apron with water from the sink. When she washes the carefully selected cosmetics from my face, I feel like I could at least try to cry, if I hadn't forgotten how to years ago.

"Your Uncle is getting The Indian Doctor out of that Cadillac you bought us," Auntie Bob announces as she breezes through the back door. My grandmother's sister had her hair cut short as a girl at Pucaseko Indian Boarding School, and everybody from Wewoka to Okmulgee has called her "Bob" ever since. Auntie Bob sucks her teeth, "Gaaaaaw, Birdie, you still look like a glamorous singing star. We wouldn't have no idea of how sick you was if we hadn't seen you fall out on the color TV over and over again. Your uncle taped it. Good thing he figured out that sophisticated color TV you sent us in time."

Welcome back to Creek Nation, Birdie Marvelous. "Good thing, Auntie Bob."

"Come to look at you twice, you do look a trifle puny," Auntie Bob reflects.

Granny Estomahe concurs. "Too skinny. Good thing The Indian Doctor is here."

Strands of silver shake as Auntie Bob turns her head. Auntie Bob and her husband spent their lives next door to my grandparents. Even back before Granddaddy Estomahe passed away, it was always pretty challenging to tell who really lived where.

Auntie Bob hollers for my uncle, who is coming up the walkway with The Indian Doctor. I watched my granddaddy Estomahe pour that walkway, then I printed my tiny hands into its rectangles. While I slept that night, Granddaddy Estomahe smoothed every trace of my palms away, as if I had never been.

I peer out of the kitchen doorway. Granny Estomahe is making a Red Carpet welcome for The Indian Doctor. He appears to be a big man, made out of commodities. Life in Nashville has taught me to look at a man's shoes, and The Indian Doctor's are sneakers. Granny Estomahe makes a fuss like Loretta Lynn and Halle Berry have both come to call on us on the same afternoon, at the same time.

I had been expecting a wizened elder. What has arrived seems more like a kid. The Indian Doctor might as well be a two-year-old. His designer jeans and hip-hop-inspired shirt fall a far cry from the ribbon shirts and cotton patchwork worn by the Stomp Dance singers and dancers. If this is what passes for *miccos* and medicine men these days, I feel vaguely doomed.

"Meet my *osuswv*, Doctor. *Fuscate Estomahe* is her name. Redbird Marvelous. We all call her Birdie," Granny Estomahe is holding The Indian Doctor's hand. The Indian Doctor smiles broadly, as if he grins during all of the hours of the day, except for the ones when he is sleeping.

"Maybe you've seen her singing on the color TV?" Auntie Bob suggests.

"For sure," answers The Indian Doctor. His voice booms in a way that sounds as if something is about to happen. "'Stonko, Birdie? I have all your songs on my iPod."

Only good home training prevents me from lying down on the floor and staying there until my change comes.

III.   MEHEWV (TRUST)

"I have shoes older than you are," I inform The Indian Doctor. Granny Estomahe and Auntie Bob serve up *sofkee* in the kitchen. My uncle is seeing about the air in the tires of the Cadillac. Since Granddaddy Estomahe passed away, my uncle does the chores of two men.

The Indian Doctor pulls both of his eyebrows together and folds his bottom lip into his upper one. For a second, until I loathe myself for noticing it, I am intrigued by the beautiful bow that dips into the flesh of his top lip. The Indian Doctor shrugs.

"You may have some, but if you do, they don't fit," The Indian Doctor replies. He has styling gel in his hair. Only the fact that The Indian Doctor wears glasses even begins to redeem him. Even after I consider his glasses, I am irritated past the point of being polite. "What?"

The Indian Doctor gazes down at my feet. "You may have shoes that are older than I am," he explains, "but since I am 30 and you are 39, those old shoes won't fit your feet anymore. Your feet have grown since you were nine years old." He nods. Twice. A long time seems to pass between each rising and lowering of his head. There is a crescent-shaped slice scarred into the side of his bronze chin.

My fingers reach toward his chin before I can stop them. I do drop them, but only after my fingertips find that The Indian Doctor is surprisingly warm.

"What happened there?" I ask. I am fully aware that I deserve for The Indian Doctor to insist that I mind my own business.

"I used to throw hands now and again." The Indian Doctor pauses, then starts to unzip his duffel bag. Faded, army green, the duffel's zipper sounds like a train clacking down a long stretch of Oklahoma track. Once, when we were little girls, my cousin Virginia and I climbed into the bleak box of a cargo train in Okmulgee and rode until the sun traded places with the beginnings of the moonlight. My breath catches in my throat as I remember the parade of trees and trailers, tinted gray in the waning sunlight. Maybe we were the parade, since Virginia and I were the ones who were passing by.

"Nice. Next, you're going to tell me you've been to prison."

The Indian Doctor's hands rummage inside the duffel bag. "I've done my time. Learned some strong medicine from elders in my cellblock." The Indian Doctor looks up from his bag. His eyes are somewhere between then and now, until he looks right at me. "Learned my lesson, too."

I am tired, as if I have run on for a long time.

IV.   EKKUCE (SMOKE)

I open my eyes in Granny Estomahe's dim bedroom. The shades are drawn, as if somebody has taken ill. Granny Estomahe wrings her hands one over the other, again and again, as if invisible worry beads fill her fingers.

"Birdie, you fell out on the floor," Auntie Bob pats my hand as she makes things plain. "Your uncle and The Indian Doctor carried you in here." My poor uncle. Someday, I hope to ask him if ever he meant to be the man of the house … twice. "Something must be done, Birdie, so The Indian Doctor is going to do it."

"If you'll let me," The Indian Doctor crafts each syllable with concentration. "I will sing my medicine songs to heal you." His words have pillows of silence between them, every one big enough to lay a whole thought on. Pillows. I feel Granny Estomahe's feather pillows raising my head. Redbird's head on Yellowbird's feathers. We belong to Panther Clan, but this whole family is filled with birds.

V. HELESWV (MEDICINE)

You are Creek.
Your Indian Doctor is singing.
You shall not want.
You have plenty of sofkee.
You shake shells at the Stomp grounds,
Wrap your soul in patchwork and ribbons.
When you walk through the valley of the Trail of Tears,
You have no fear.
The RedStick Warriors are with you.
War clubs and panthers, they comfort you.
You spread cornbread in the presence of your enemies,
Soldiers who have run on a long time,
Long in the tooth,
Shortsighted with a rifle.
You pour red Kool-Aid and sweet tea.
Your cup runs over.
It is just a jelly jar anyway.
Your dear granny never throws them away.

Surely, what is sacred will follow you all the days of your life.
And you will dwell in Creek Nation forever.

VI.   ROYANKUCE (MOURNFUL)

My shoulder lands first against the cold, concrete floor first.

"You stay there," Virginia whispers. She is my first cousin, my sister, Indian way, and I love her. So, I listen. I listen when the springs creak as Virginia assumes my shape in my bed in the Blessed Kateri Dormitory at Pucaseko Indian Boarding School. I listen while the springs scream as Father Harris moves, up-down, up-down, on top of a form that he believes to be mine.

VII.   ENOKKE (SICK)

Virginia asks me to sing. "Sing, Baby Bird," she sighs. She says that she forgets to remember whenever I sing. "Someday, Baby Bird," Auntie Bob's only daughter proclaims, "you gonna sing on television. And all over the whole wide world."

When I do, I buy her a house, across the street from our grandparents. It is as close as I can get her.

One night in August, she lights match after match, then lies down on her bed and watches, while she burns underneath the flames.

VIII.   TOTKV (FIRE)

The count begins with a column of winters,
manifests in a chill, the damp after rain.
My contagious pain is a stained-glass fortress.

I cannot come any closer, because I cannot come.
So, I run.
Roll my regrets into paper and light them,
pour shame into glasses until they overflow,
recall much more than I am admitting
in a confessional created from scars,
where the way of the priest's sears like lye in my mouth.
Now, I resent the taste of coriander.

IX. CVFEKNE (HEALTHY)

"Am I dying?" I whisper. Granny Estomahe rearranges the feather pillows supporting my head.

"You were," Auntie Bob shares from the side of the bed. She is tucking me into the sheets. "The Indian Doctor helped you sing out something in your soul that was killing you. So, you were dying, but you ain't now."

X. FEKE (HEART)

I see The Indian Doctor later, at Walmart, where you are never too surprised to see any Indian.

The Indian Doctor stands behind me in the check-out line. He slides a heart-shaped box, covered in slick red-and-white-striped paper, over the scanner. He places a folded twenty on the conveyer belt.

"Those chocolates are for you," says The Indian Doctor, as if nothing strange is happening, even for us Oklahoma Indians. "Happy Valentine's Day."

Every time I eat one of those chocolates, I sing.

I finish the final piece of candy on Friday. As I swallow sugar, The Indian Doctor knocks on Granny Estomahe's front door.

"Be my wife." The Indian Doctor swirls each word as if we are continuing a conversation that both of us ought to know about, but only one of us does.

"Why?" I surprise myself that I am not surprised.

The Indian Doctor holds out his hand. There is a leather bag in it. I take his gift.

"Because you can sing."

"I didn't win that Grammy."

The Indian Doctor groans. "Not *that* kind of singing. That's for white people. I mean Indian singing. Singing for healing."

"I thought you had all my music on your iPod."

"Well, yeah. For riding in the truck. For cruising to Seminole or Proctor for a hog fry or a wild onion dinner. Not for medicine."

"I'd make a terrible Indian Doctor's wife."

The Indian Doctor takes off his glasses and cleans them on his t-shirt. "No, you'd make a terrible *preacher's* wife," The Indian Doctor corrects me, "on account of how you wear too much makeup and don't know your Bible all that well. You'd make a great Indian Doctor's wife."

"I know my Bible just fine," I retort. "And my makeup is perfect. I am on makeup *commercials*. Plenty of people think I look *amazing*."

The Indian Doctor muses for a minute. His thoughts take their own kind of time and definitely make their own kind of sense. "Plenty of people think you look *expensive*. I think you look more amazing the way Creator made you. As for the Bible, I don't care. I like our old ways."

Granny Estomahe turns off the kitchen faucet. She and Auntie Bob are listening to what The Indian Doctor has to say. Since they do not interrupt us, I know that they approve.

"Look, I appreciate you coming to cure me and all, but you're like ... a kid ...."

"No, I'm *not*," The Indian Doctor cuts me off mid-sentence. "I'm a grown man. And you're a grown woman. That makes us grown folks. And grown folks can do whatever they like. If you don't mind and I don't mind and Creator don't mind, then there's not any other reason why you shouldn't be my woman. My *grown* woman."

Chairs scrape across the kitchen floor. Granny Estomahe and Auntie Bob move closer to the doorway to hear us more clearly. I know better than to leave The Indian Doctor standing on the steps outside, literally putting our business out in the street. Yet, I cannot let him in. Strangely, I cannot think of telling him to go.

"You know, I have a good career going," I start to say.

"Your career 'bout got you killed," the Indian Doctor smiles at me. "And you're gonna tell me next that I don't have a career at all. But I do. I'm a doctor. And a lotta ladies would like to marry a doctor."

"You sure know a lot." I sound meaner than I intended.

The Indian Doctor chuckles. "I know you can sing. And I know Creator didn't give you that gift just so you can shake your hind end in music videos. I know sickness can be healed when you sing. And I know you can sing with me." He winks at me. "Trust me, I'm a doctor."

I laugh, in spite of myself. The Indian Doctor grins at me. In the kitchen, my uncle comes through the back door. Granny Estomahe and Auntie Bob hush my uncle when he wants to know why they are letting The Indian Doctor stand outside in the wind.

"Tell you what," the Indian Doctor begins to back down the front steps. "I gotta doctor a patient in Muscogee tomorrow. Ride with me over that way. If Creator gives you a healing song to sing, you marry me. If He don't, you go back to being famous, same as you ever was." The Indian Doctor gestures to the leather bag in my hand. "Bring that with you."

I open the bag as his truck roars away. A turtle shell rattle fits as if it was made for my hand. And all of the handle is beaded with red birds. I am not surprised to enter Granny Estomahe's kitchen and discover that all of my relatives are smiling.

XI. AFVCKE (JOYFUL)

The Indian Doctor is singing. He is singing song after song, for hour after hour, over a patient whose limbs are twisted and swollen with water. Fluid rises and falls within her lungs, ebbing just long enough to allow her to gasp in a macabre rattle. Weeping blends with her daughters' murmured prayers.

Sweat streams down The Indian Doctor's face and saturates his shirt. His eyes, shut against every distraction from curing this sickness and disease, show signs of deep shadows and fatigue. We had arrived as the sun ruled the middle of the sky. Night overcame this day hours ago.

"Nakete?" A faint mumble crosses the patient's lips. "What is this?"

The Indian Doctor opens his eyes. He raises his rattle. His voice cracks as he strains to sing another song that will help the woman to heal the rest of the way. I stand up and cross her bedroom. I lay my hand on The Indian Doctor's shoulder. For the rest of our lives, I help him sing.

CONCEIVED SEED

Creator,
Nights when the beat of a heart is the drum,
When Warriors rise and Stomp with the moon,
We rise, too,
Open our shawls and promise plenty.
None will go hungry, be lost or unloved.
Days when the sun shines down on Ceremony,
We stand strong, too.
Moccasins Stomp Dance under the sky,
Firmly plant us in the earth.
Life lasts forever, when we honor You first.

THOUSANDS OF MILLIONS

An urge to rage is the first temptation.
Bite into the shards of your heart like glass,
Ask Andrew Jackson
To battle,
Rattle the names of The Trail of Tears,
Sand Creek,
RedSticks,
Till they strike fear.

When your enemy ain't looking, pick up a pencil,
Stencil the language in beats and rhymes,
Time for a flute and some southern style singing,
Ringing against racism,
Bringing us home.

WINTER COUNT

For Duane Brayboy-Williams

NOKOSE

Everybody called my uncles the "Sons of Thunder." They cut a wide swath thru the South, fists flying, panties dropping, shot calling and money balling.

Then I arrived. "We thought what if she grows up to marry a Skin just like us?" Uncle O told me. "Then, we'd have to kill that joker and do time." So, they changed. How much? "If somebody messes with you," Uncle Sugar grins, "we won't kill him. We'll just make him wish we had."

CUFE

"No matter how much meat you feed it, a wolf will always run from your table back to the woods," my granddaddy used to say. "Wild boys ain't much different. Choose wisely."

LVMHE

"I voted," my other granddaddy used to say. "I been voting since I been a man. Wrote in Osceola, Billy Jack, Crazy Horse, and Quanah Parker." He said that every time he voted, but we already knew he voted Democrat every time.

ESTE-CATE

"What's that?" I asked my granddaddy. "It's a Treaty," he answered as he picked me up and set me on his knee. "Treaties are promises. And

20

it's a very bad thing to be a breaker of promises. They break a treaty, they don't just answer to a courthouse, they have to answer to Edoda and our ancestors." Then he read me the Treaty of New Echota. Out loud. Every word. I was four years old.

MICCO

"Ain't just weapons that win a war," my granddaddy, a WWII VET, told me. "Everybody thinks you win a war with your weapons, or with your strategy. They think that's where you win a war, but it ain't. Where you win a war is your friends, the folks who fight alongside you. You can't win a war by yourself .... Allies matter."

AYO

"We gon' talk about this later," my granddaddy used to say when any of us got into trouble, "but we gon' fix it first." Mercy triumphs over judgment.

HENEHA

Twelve times Crimson Harjo has kept me alive. "Sometimes I think I can feel you, even when you're afar off," he says, "but doctors said after 90 days all of your blood was your own. But I sometimes I think that during those 90 days, my heart was helping yours beat." He's calmly driving. I'm stunned to hear him say so many words at once. My granddaddy used to say, "there's all kinds of ways to tell somebody you love 'em. Never knew a Native who needed to use words."

TUSTINIGEE

Unity is our strength. My granddaddy used to say, "no such thing as a Black NDN, a South American NDN or a White NDN. You're either NDN or you're not, and if you are NDN, there's work to be done ... get to getting."

TOTKE

"Watch the Whirlwinds, but wed a Warrior," my granddaddy told me at the first powwow we went to after my coming of age ceremony. I think of that every time I watch men's traditional. I think that's why I so love that category.

TENETKE

My granddaddy used to say, "Don't ever tell your enemy that his arrow did its work. Don't holler, don't show pain. Keep fighting, win and walk off. Make your enemy worry that his arrow might have missed. He'll think twice before shooting at you again."

HECE

"If a pretty girl decides to fall in love with a knife ... she best be sure not to cut herself when she kisses the blade, "My granddaddy used to say. He was talking about the kind of men that some folks call "Bad Boys."

HVRESSE

"Stand around being NDN long enough and you'll find yourself in the middle of a family reunion," my granddaddy told me in the Amtrak train station one time. Wasn't ten minutes before a slice of pound cake and sweet tea proved him right.

HERUSE

"This whole family's too damn good looking for our own good," my granddaddy used to say ... "and, that's a good thing, cause if you'uns gone stay in this family, you best be pretty or you best be useful."

ETO

You know what my Uncle Clarence did? Back when he fell in love with my granddaddy's sister, it was illegal for a Southern White person to marry a Native person. So he gave up White Privilege, lived under Jim Crow, even worked for Civil Rights. He Stomp Danced and stayed happily wed to Aunt Pauline for 60 years. Native Elders at the BIA are talking about what a good Native man he was. I start to correct them, but then I realize they're right.

HOKTE

Crimson Harjo is a Creek, but on account of his mama and my grandmama being best friends and Uncle Sugar and him being best friends, when Crimson's Mama married a new man and moved out West, he just stayed here with us. He and Sugar got to stay home from first grade on the day I was born. "Looky here Crim," Uncle Sugar told Crimson, "a lil' baby Creek. Ain't she pretty?"

According to Granddaddy, Crimson Harjo leaned over and told me something in my ear. It's the only thing other than "happy birthday," "Merry Christmas" or "sugar here?" that anybody knows for sure he ever said to me. The happiest day of my life was the day he told me what it was.

TAFV

Grampa Brice is my granddaddy 's baby brother. He walks the white path, married to a non-Native. My granddaddy was a hard core traditional. I'm surprised when Grampa Brice asks me to sing Cherokee hymns. "I want to hear what my Mama sounded like again, Baby Girl. I'm forgetting."

HELE

"You always got to have that one unsaved friend," my granddaddy used to say. "Church folks gotta repent or whatever they do. So you gotta keep the Traditionals, the Warriors, the wild ones around you. They know, they ain't scared and they ain't gotta ask permission or forgiveness."

KATCV

Granddaddy explained things when I was tiny. "Making a picture of me, you need the black crayon for my hair and red one for my skin," he said as he drew himself. "To make a picture of you, you need ALL the crayons!" I giggled. Granddaddy hugged me, "Osda, Honeygirl. The prettiest things in life need all the crayons to color."

NERE

My granddaddy used to say, "Never fight a man till you know how far he's willing to go. And if you ain't willing to go that far or farther—fight him another day."

ECHOTA

You know, my granddaddy never would say "goodbye" to me. He always said, "love you forever and all the days after." He meant every word. When I say it, I mean every word, too.

CULTURE CHRONICLES
For my Uncle Don Birchfield

Our enemies tell this lie to the masses,
Claim we dine on bread and roses.
While others suffer, punch time cards,
They say we eat our tithes and don't pay taxes.

Here is the truth, I don't care how they tell it.
Columbus was lost and in need of a compass.
He lacked a conscience, which makes it worse.
Once a year, we stay home, treat unconquered nations
To the chance to surpass us, get ahead for a day.
All courtesy of a man so brazen,
He refused to believe he could fall off the world.
Swollen hands, splayed feet, the smell of onions,
He claimed this land in the name of his color,
More for the sake of his soul than ours.

I'd say we were honest to a fault,
Telling those Pilgrims they could stay.
No one owned the earth anyway.
It grew squash for all, regardless of color.
We told them our numbers and our ways.
Our hearts were such glass, they were broken by smallpox.

One lie we told, and we're not a bit sorry.
We started the rumor that the earth was flat.

We came by night to trouble the Vikings,
Shook them sober with rattle and bone,
Made their Greenland disappear,
Sent survivors home with the fear

That maybe they could sail over the edge.
Stay home, we warned, don't tempt Leviathan.
We had peace and quiet for quite a few years.

POWWOW PROVERBS

For my Uncle Jay Red Eagle

Uncle Jay calls me Princess, even though I've no crown,
Says "Think twice before trading their gold rings for your blankets.
Remember the rift between whiskey and water.
Whiskey makes mistakes, talks to strangers.
Clean water keeps its distance.
Why brave the bitter of whiskey?
Spit while snake-handling?
Play Truth-Or-Dare?
Stay home, choose our Warriors.
Let them find other Queens."

RED BIRD RISING

For my Sister, Robin

My sister went driving through love in the winter,
Took a wrong turn and drove headlong,
Into his fists of thunder and lightning.
A broken promise made everything wrong.
Now,
Some trust in horses,
I trust in dance.
Fearless of flying,
Spinning,
Leaping,
Into the reservation sky.
When I dance,
She dances, too.

SECRET THINGS, THINGS REVEALED

"Ain't no mystery who's Indian," Granddaddy says, as the smoke from his unfiltered Camel cigarette wreathes his WII Veteran hat. "You're either Indian or you're not, and if you **are** Indian, there's work to be done ... get to getting."

One of Granddaddy's older sisters plunged a slice of glass into her thigh and dragged it down, rather than let a white man rape her. Tormented by the sight of her bleeding to death before him, that man signed all his land over to all Granddaddy's parents, before he slit his own throat with a razor. This is why I want to be the wife of only one man. I come from women who would choose death before dishonor.

"You know the difference between white folks and Indians? Go in white folks' houses and they've got pictures of people they don't know, doing things they don't know about and places they've never been. They call all that Art. Go into Indians' houses and every wall is filled up with photos of people we love. Go to somebody's house and look at their walls," Granddaddy says. "You'll know who belongs on the rolls."

I was conceived a Holy Thing. Grief Fever took my parents' first children before they came to the light. As my bereaved parents despaired of ever holding a living child in their arms, my ten uncles cut into theirs. Pouring blood into the Sacred Fire, they asked for a child and promised to protect it. I arrived soon after, this family's first Shellshaker in a generation. I am my parents' daughter, but I am my uncles' baby, too.

"It's God's grace to be a princess in a family of men." Granddaddy smiles at me. "This has its advantages."

My Cousin Ty Ty Osceola is beautiful. It should be hilarious that everyone calls him Ty Ty now, instead of Tiger, just because I named him that when I was a baby. Nobody laughs at him though. He is a Marine.

"I took that picture because I saw you and Tiger and O sleeping, and I thought I have the most beautiful children." Granddaddy sighs as the ash burns in long lines on his cigarette. "And then, since it was two hours past sunrise, I thought I also might have the laziest."

Palen Harjo, my childhood playmate, is a Marine now. He tapes our prom picture in his helmet each time he goes to war. I ask him, "why? Do you think I am good luck?"

"Ain't no such thing as luck," he chuckles. "I just think you look real pretty."

"When God is trying to give you something," Granddaddy explains. "All you have to do is say yes."

This is how it happens. My Cousin Gisgi has words with a white guy, who ends up badly beaten later that night. When the Law picks him up, my Cousin Chowder, my childhood playmate Palen Harjo, Uncle Sugar, his best friend Crimson, Cousin Minoxody Harjo and Cousin Ty Ty each drive over to the jail in their trucks and confess. They do this one by one, all night long, until the bartender finally tells the Law that Gisgi is blameless. When I see him at Walmart the next week, the sheriff says he's never seen anything quite like our family before. "You see, Sheriff," I tell him, "if somebody in this family is going through Hell, he doesn't have to go there by himself."

"You don't have to tell everything you know, Honeygirl," Granddaddy tells me, twirling his cigarette between his long fingers.

If a relative texts "forever" to our phones, everybody has to text back, "and one day." Then, we must all stop what we are doing and go to where they are and do whatever it takes to rescue them. That's the only reason any of us have ever been to Raccoon Gap, KY and Hell, AZ and International Falls, MN in the same year.

"There's such a thing as Incidents," Granddaddy taps his fingers on his knee. "Ain't no such thing as Accidents."

The Harjo boys are different. Fearless. Ajenna, Hajenna, Minoxody, Alenna and John Horse. They are bloodthirsty. They like this about themselves. They are tremendous Marines. They like this about themselves, too.

"Bloodthirsty? Ain't nothing wrong with any of my grandsons," Granddaddy muses. He pauses, fondles his silver Zippo lighter. "'Cept the Corps taught 'em to kill and it taught 'em to like it. Growing a garden, sitting in service ... once you've got an appetite for blood, water ain't nothing."

When I arrive at Cousin Chowder's, he is sobbing under the bed, swaddled in a nest of pillows and Pendletons. July 4 fireworks don't set him off, he's expecting them, but random fireworks on July 6 or 7 do. Too much time in Iraq makes him wary of wars and rumors of war. His little dog is sleeping next to him. As I climb under the bed, I figure I might as well, too.

"This I know for sure, Honeygirl," Granddaddy promises, "love will come and save you."

THE REMEMBRANCE OF RACHEL

Lifeblood flows first,
Water last,
A measure of time,
An acre of dread,
Bred in the bone and the desire of nations.

When longing turns evil,
Casts eyes toward the Rez,
Says, while you build empires,
Your heart will never be fed.

This is the answer,
The only reply,
Dance.
Sing songs of snow and salmon,
Tell stories of the old ones and their ways,
Pray,
In days filled with dry meat and rain,
Pain bound by cedar,
Broken by sage
Rage redeemed
By children wearing elders' names.

SAINTS IN LIGHT

After the Long Walk,
Trailing tears,
Creeks came to Indian Territory,
Asked, "Nakete? Where is the water?"
Answered by silence and the absence of rain,
Fingered dry clay and fell dead in pain.
Every reservation brick is baked ash and bone.
Now,
Wet earth and rivers flood all our dreams.
Allotments and treaties fill our waking hours.
In this dry, thirsty land where no water is,
Blood is money.
The currency is rain.

Nakete: "What is it?" in Creek

THE SUBSTANCE OF HOPE

Multitudes of people, crying,
Moaning for manna and pleading for quail,
Shouting, reaching, pushing, shoving.
Salt and sugar, cornmeal and lard,
Eating is everything, pass your basket,
It's Ceremony, this gift of loaves and fishes.

THE DOWRY OF DAWN

I sing you to me.
Drummers who know what it means to make time
Rhyme
Run into blankets and beats and find
Lines
Of Stomp Dance songs.
I sing you to me.

I sing you to me.
Warriors and Protectors who know this is not Eden
Even
Fight ghosts and shadows.
Peace
Costs you your dreams.
I sing you to me.

I sing you to me.
Men of medicine who know there is no sin
When
Sage and cedar, ginseng and weel
Heal
Burns left by fire and brimstone.
I sing you to me.

I sing you to me.
Chiefs who ponder on your beds
Heads
Of states of gaming and mind
Find
When you call, Creator answers.
I sing you to me.

I sing you to me.
Factors, men of the open hand
Trading wisdom, wealth and land.
Sand
Wiped from the eyes
Lies
Revealed and banished.
I sing you to me.

I sing you to me.
Long-fingered hunters who draw back the bow,
Know
How to stop a heart with a prayer,
There
With you is always plenty.
I sing you to me.

I sing you to me.
Men created from red earth and red clay
Who know how to work and who know how to stay
I ask Creator to make a way
For you to answer my song.

A Thousand Times More

Our women,
We dance
To show faith,
That our men will come home from life's war.

We bend our knees,
Swing our shawls,
Honor Creator by lifting feather fans,
Thankful our Warriors come home victorious,
Come home to tribal dances and the answer to drums.
Come home to the revolution.
Come home to Jubilee.

WORTHY PORTION
What Crimson Totke Harjo Told Me

White boys sleep through your screaming.
It is us
Red men
Who sing you back to sleep
Rock you until you remember to cry
Wet our mouths with salt and water
Kissing the monsters out of your memories.
When you sleep,
We slay them,
And
Give you their spirits as proof.

White boys shush your singing.
It is us
Skins
Who answer your body
Hold you until you hear drums
Touch you with flute music under the stars
Denying you nothing
When you sigh,
We love you,
And
Give you our hearts as trophies.

White boys share none of your suffering.
It is us,
Este-cate,
Who pray you into wholeness
Steal you boldly back from Death
Salvage the shards of your heart

Stroke your hand to remind you to live.
When you ask us to go to war for you,
We do.
We give you our lives as promises.

Este-cate: Creek words for "Red people"

ONE HEART

What Crimson Totke Harjo Told Me Again

This family,
We are losing our women
To the arms
To the lives
Of men
With ice instead of eyes
Who fill their lives with imitations of us,
With our art,
Our drums,
Our women.

We take you back by moonlight,
Bruise your mouths with impatient tongues
Denied too long to linger.
You must remember us by day,
Long for us by night.
Our fingers wet with honey,
Our heartbeat under Pendleton blankets,
Our bodies two-step dancing in the way life meant for us.

In the violence of the sun,
This family,
This family of men,
We lose our women again.
This time they stay gone.
The Time of Life
Soul Love happens first in the spirit,
Moves sweetly southbound,
Takes root in the heart.
Ask me how I know,
So,

I can tell tales of mountains and valleys,
How I looked back and became a pillar,
Until you came.
Spun sugar from salt,
Now I will stay.
I am well-watered, come with me,
And see
How two become one and angels speak,
As manna showers us on command.
Make room for my halo in your bed.
That said,
Your words fill my heart with blood and fire.
Desire, you might call it, if you give it a name,
Leave shame to Judas, Andrew Jackson and Cain.
I pray,
You bring rain.

MERMAID PRINCESS

The swirl of the sea, in an ocean of smoke,
Stirs Siren songs that make sailors see Mermaids.
Mermaids?
Yes, even after Eden,
Since winter rain froze and hearts grew hard,
Scarred,
Left on the shore,
Wanting more,
Than the season of salt rising with every tide.
Mermaids beckon,
Buoyant on seafoam,
Promising wanderers
They are home.

NAMING CEREMONIES

Our feasts carry
Stories,
Songs,
Scars
Toward
Stars,
Stomp Dances,
Brush arbors,
Churches,
Where
Each supper is a slice of light
In nights,
Rife
With
The life of our tribes.

SIGNS FOLLOWING ON THE TRAIL OF TEARS

Sorrow at dawn, again at dusk,
Grinds our insides, knots our bellies.
Pangs fingerwoven from the mourning for meat.
Our cheeks draw close together, water, sour with dry flour.

Some mornings, we wake weeping,
Cup our souls within our hands,
Pour our spirits out of our lips.
With each step we trudge on this Trail of Tears.

A ration of joy would redeem our lives.
We crave the crumbs white soldiers disdain,
Pray they, on purpose, leave handfuls behind.
What they esteem lightly enlightens our eyes.

Nights make us ache for when we had plenty,
Were prosperous people, our steps oiled with butter.
There were grapes in that land it took two to carry.
Then, there were not.
That was Canaan.
We know it.
Memory satisfies one kind of hunger.

THE PENANCE OF GENOCIDE
For Gil and all the Ancestors

There is no sorrow like unto my sorrow.
Swathed in leather,
Seasoned with beads,
I need
To know
I do not come to Stomp alone.
I hear other shells besides my own
As the Spirits join
Bind their songs into one mind
Stir sacred fire and remind
That the revolt of the heart begins with a portrait,
Lines inked in the parchment of maps
The promise of gold and a succulent dowry
Weighed and metered in treaties and flour,
Spun from the blood of Warriors and Mothers
And Brothers,
Spattered,
Patterned
Against rocks and boulders
Mortar
For bricks that build nations.

What Abigail Knew

Warriors with understanding
Stand
When others run,
Hum the songs of the Saints as they turn on their beds.
Instead,
They ascertain,
Remain
Steadfast in perilous times,
And know what we ought to do.

Osceola knew.
You do, too.
Like Geronimo, Joshua , Popay and Peter,
Leaders lit
By a guiding light.
Fight the good fight,
Till Kingdom come.

PHOENIX

For Cousin Kathy

Tendrils of flowers,
The hours curl,
Add lines to circles, and patterns unfurl.
You, the artist, make sense of it all,
Call worlds into being,
Cast a pall,
Over tyranny,
A remedy
Rendered and framed
In flames.

REPROACH REMOVED

Older than this New Nation,
Yet your tongues lie in our mouths,
Leave tastes of lye,
Each sigh,
Like bloodlines twisted,
Vines dyed and tied.

Wine turned into water,
A tie that binds,
One spirit too many,
After which we find
When we summon angels,
Demons come.
Drunk on the poison of genocide,
They will not be satisfied,
Till there is no land,
        No water,
        No later

For all of us

At all.

King of Saints

Unconquered
By conquistadors,
Crusaders,
Collectors of souls,
No.
Then
When
Under the sun, you cast your shadow,
The smile of God from God,
Light from light,
Not begotten, but made,
In accordance with our scriptures,
Of corn,
Beads,
Arrows,
Wood.
All so good,
We find honey in the desert.

THE ALCHEMY OF MISCEGENATION

Crossing blood,
Rinsing my soul,
I meet a masked brother,
Raccoon,
Panning for shine in the river.
Foil, fool's gold, twist,
Straw spun into gold.
Sufficient treasure
For this small miner.

Our ancestors were carried off moons ago,
So,
Never finding home haunts us most,
The remnants of souls in the reflection of deeds.
Never joining hearts haunts us second,
No redemption for bad heart investments.

Raccoon,
It's as good as bankrupt,
This word
"Race."

AUNT LAHOMA SINGS THE BOARDING SCHOOL BLUES

In class that morning,
I learned about Icarus.
I sat with captive children,
Forced to study.
Seduced by chocolate,
I listened,
But I already knew
What it means to lose your wings,
To fall from grace.
You can no longer fly.

I make archangels cry,
As I long for cedar,
Miss the shooting of stars over my stomp ground,
Lack patchwork skirts,
Ache for the braids I wore like a crown.

When the nuns lash my back,
I sing to myself
That
I am no fool.

I once was loved.

PANTHER PRAYERS

When I walk again on the old paths, I'll say no,
Whisper winter instead of yes,
Save my hope this drought,
Spare my faith this famine.
When I walk again on the old paths,
I'll not be caged.
My enemies will know nothing of grace.

The Calvary of Enrollment

"He was there, and then he ran away," Sgili accused.

The people felt troubled. Tawodi, Hawk, was one of the strongest warriors, and the thought of his heart fainting in battle pained the hearts of the Echota People.

Warriors, hunters, and mothers murmured among themselves. Tawodi was there and then he was not there. Tawodi had been seen and then he had not been seen. Gisgi and Yona vowed that they had fought beside Tawodi. Trouble, Doubt, and Almost claimed that only his hawk-shaped shadow had entered the battle. Finally, the Speaker of the Warriors commanded quiet.

Tawodi stood silent, wrapped in a woven blanket.

"You were there?" the Speaker of the Warriors asked, knowing and not knowing his bravest fighter's answer.

Tawodi stayed silent. The people gasped as he opened the blanket and let it fall to the grass. Ribbons of blood wrapped around his powerful arms and legs, while blood swam down from a gash in his side, mingling with salt and sweat and water. The measure of a hatchet seeped blood beneath his collarbone.

The people never doubted Tawodi again. After all, they were there when he showed them his wounds.

REDEEMING THE TIME
For the Boarding School Survivors

When survivors meet
On the streets
Of Denver,
Memphis,
Chicago,
Cleveland,
Anywhere else but home,
If they are not known,
This is how they trade
Names,
Clans,
DNA
Open their blankets, then look away
To show
They know one another's pain
Heartbeats say all that they need to say.

CARLISLE CHORUS

Boarding school haircuts,
Ira Hayes,
Pangs of hunger,
Dresses of gray,
Disappointed missionaries say
Last call for Assimilation
For Heaven,
For Termination.

Every child left behind
In orange jumpsuits, trailers, or a colonized mind.

We find aches of every kind,
Hearts in pieces
Seep weeping vibes.

Run and tell that,
Pratt,
While we pour oil and wine in the wounds
Which ooze,
The proof of the wars we fought in.

THE GOSPEL ACCORDING TO HULDAH

I hear the stars singing.
I run to meet You.
My feet print clay.
I speak what you say.
Now,
My hands multiply milk instead of loaves and fishes.
My world is filled with virtue, not fools.
My steps are spread with butter.
Oil pours from rocks as I talk.
Honey on my tongue is Your Amen.

ANSWER OF PEACE

I am reading.
My mind makes sense of dots and dashes.
I find whole lifetimes in lines and angles.
My moccasins stomp through cyberspace.

I hear the tongue of those in charge
In the mouths of those who know better
Until the end of the trail is
The spark of revival.

I am learning.
My fingers bind broken treaties
And battered hearts
With bandages woven from nouns,
Verbs,
Adverbs,
And an occasional gerund.
I apply participles to speed healing.

I feed the people
Then burn sage for them
Green Corn Ceremony, wherever we are,
Love writes our names among the stars.

STAR CLAN SONG

Joshua, Judges, Ruth.
That's how they say it goes.
Craft a calf out of gold and see how your life changes.
Rahab is the exception, Tamar, a fluke.
You'd best mind your manners and keep your soul clean.
Or you might be swept away by floods,
Pillared in salt,
Burned by brimstone.

Yet, I cannot surrender
My nations,
My name.
I will not unpack my tongue and hand it over.
I am serving.
The alphabet girl who molds sticks and spheres,
Making them into land claims and letters.
I claim as a trophy this thing called writing.
On good days,
I shake shells
And
Read out loud.

Kituwah Mound and the Great Smoky Mountains
Fuel my fire.
I watch my legacy burn into my moccasins,
My heart and my beadwork.
Around the slope of the flames,
My relatives dance.

THE MIRACLE OF MAYBE

John Williams, Reverend Father
(Puritan clergyman John Williams and his family
were captured during a raid on Deerfield,
Massachusetts. Williams and his son were rescued
from their Native captors, yet his daughter, Eunice,
was adopted by Mohawks and married Arosen, a
Native man. Offered the opportunity to leave her
Native relatives, she refused by saying simply,
"Maybe not.")

All of my dreams end in my daughter.
I rescue her hundreds of times in my sleep.
Only then, I am courageous.
Only then, I am cunning,
Running towards clouds of locusts and honey,
And money.
Wielding the jawbone of a donkey,
I release Eunice from the heathens.
I have my reasons
For shouting down walls with the salt of my sermon.
My victories end with the taking of heads.

When I wake, there is only Patience,
Our weary mule.
Her jawbone is better left as it is.

My new bride barely moves in the night.
She has no memories made by arrows.
The remains of my children rest in straight lines,
Whine for Eunice.
I fear now she dreams in circles.
I preach and I pace and I pray for the masses,
Hear myself called redeemed by Mather,

Rather
Than my foes, who cannot smell brimstone.
They have no more dread of Hell than of cotton or weeds,
Or me.
In spite of my ecclesiastical tantrums,
The only spoils of this war are phantoms.

Stephen Williams, Brother and Aspiring Redeemer

You've plenty of gall, new brother Arosen.
We were children who ruled this new world from the womb,
Like David, that man after God's own heart,
Who pleased Heav'n so much He appointed him king.
All that winning and dancing and severing heads,
Led to not being the kind of father
Who could be careful for what he sired.
They tell us you're a prince, too,
Who is vainly adorned in glass beads and hawk fathers,
Broiling the vanquished with stakes on fire,
Gorging your appetite for sisters,
Tearing open their bodies with filed teeth and tight claws,
Ripping away the purity under modest dresses,
Biting the English from the tips of their tongues,
Bloodying them with the taint of brown.
Now,
If I was born fierce, I would take your life.
An eye for an eye, I should rake you blind,
In both,
And make my father love me.
Liberating my sister,
I could make myself king.
Not being willing to hang from the trees,
Preferring not to be served in gravy,
I'd just as soon wait to inherit the kingdom,
To buy back our Eunice with hammered round silver,
Thirty pieces in jars of clay.
Until then, I despise you and curse your dust and ashes.

EUNICE WILLIAMS, CAPTIVE WIFE AND MOTHER

Kanenstenhawi, Mohawks changed my name,
But how I changed first is that my feet became wider,
Splayed and broadened set free from their shoes,
I remember my tongue thickened, too,
Liberated from speaking so much sin and judgment.

I prefer making round sounds now,
The kind that use the flat of the mouth,
Pucker the lips into the kissing of wind,
The type that cross your ears like water,
Nestle somewhere deep inside you.
I said maybe,
Yet I meant
NO.
Go.
Alone.
I am home.

A PILLOW OF STONE

Our story begins with a count made of winters,
Ends in a chill, a damp after rain.
A contagious pain is a stained-glass quarantine.
You cannot come any closer because we cannot come.
So, we run.
Roll our regrets into cedar and lose them,
Weave shame into sage until we can pray,
That we understand now more than when we were living
Under the pursuit of wisdom.
In a confessional made of scars.
Until the way of the priests leaves lye in our mouths
And we rebuke the taste of coriander
The Mercies of Heaven.

Her atonement smells of bleach,
Sometimes of fatback,
More often, of lye,
Burning tears from slanted eyes,
Falling, filling yard-sale pitchers
With sweet, red Kool-Aid, blushing sorry,
Gritty with sugar, the way he likes it,
Lukewarm, made with cold well water,
Left to sit, courting the flour,
Fried into bread,
Filled with mountain air,
And enough grease to oil a promise,
The only antidote for shame.

His remorse lights his cigarette,
He gave up fourteen years ago.
Ash leaves the color she fears love is.

Sorry helps her hang the wash,
Folds flannel and heart into lines and odd angles,
Starches his shirts with compensation,
Irons conviction in the creases of sheets.

He looks in his pocket, the left one, and finds
She sewed it back in a straight line,
With a broken needle and what's left of a thimble,
She tied a knot of good intentions.

She takes his contrite heart in her hands,
Penance made good outlasts her objections,
He lifts the blankets, murmurs for home,
Takes his place on the side she warmed.
She watches him shiver his regret.

From now on, every day is Lent.

THE MIDWIVES' HOUSES

I know how late I am.
I may be the latest woman you know,
Keeping your time and mine.
Two pulses,
Two heartbeats,
Two books of hours.

Aware, I entertain angels,
Adorned in patchwork and turbans,
They wander up the walk,
Help themselves to oatmeal.

I see glory in their faces.
I serve them.

TIMES AND SEASONS

I saved a burning bush, on the way to work.
I stopped to blow on the blaze.
The flame died, tired as I right now am.
I would be late, again,
But I paused to whisper mvto,
Thank you,
Make medicine from its charred limbs.
Truth is,
I opened my eyes at Dawn.
I could have dressed right then,
Made it in,
Yet, I walked into the river,
Wet my soul for a while.
Seasons changed in my Spirit,
I made my own time.

Mvto: "Thank you" in Creek

CheroCreek Crossing

Rez car only does
Forty miles an hour.
We could get there faster walking,
But
You yearn for hawk feathers and honor beats.

The radio works,
So
We drive all night,
Add oil as we go.

Rez car leaks and it starts to pour.
We would be drier outside,
But you dream drums,
And I dream you,
So
We stay late and sleep in the seats.
We make our own thunder.

AN ALTAR OF HORNS

In the end of days,
Prophets warn of deer,
Heading east in herds of antlers,
Orderly marching right, left, right hoof,
Covering plains and coming this way,
Rattling their throats with the names of martyrs,
Bloodying highways and broken by hunters,
Painting the grills of trucks and cars.
Enough is enough.
This has gone too far.
Away
They go.
Wise men see trouble and hide themselves,
In cellars,
In hollers,
In Stomp grounds,
In churches.
Fools take pictures.
The deer save soldiers from themselves,
Show warriors how to handle snakes.
Crush their heads with the comers of hooves,
Don't give them time to offer the apple,
Or drink poison, rather.
No matter.
These deer have a mission, they come to help.
Not since the bison have they searched for leaders,
Veterans versed in war and its rumors.
Yet there are still weapons and conflicts and fires,
Tainting the water and the land they call home.
Something must go.
Left, right, left, they claim their own.

UNEQUAL YOKE

"We are not that kind of people."
Grandmother Octie lifts her head.
"We do not kill the fatted calf,
Sever ties, break bread in half
And toss it in the road.
No,
We are not the ones
Who take fat and lives and land,
Then hold out the open hand
Demand
Your tongue, your hair, your stand
On paper, of lies, in blood."

THE SIGNET OF JUDAH

Tear the treaties, pull them to pieces,
Call a war cry, sing death songs,
Until the colonies fade and the conquistadors flee,
Wail like women, wave like water.
This is how the beginning ends.
Sins,
Written in blood and smallpox,
Etched into the skin they're in,
Until times turn,
Change,
Until the range is once again,
Home.

WHAT THE HEART WANTS

All we ever wanted,
You're All we ever wanted
And All we ever wanted
Is what we ask You for

All we ever wanted
You're All we ever wanted
And All we ever wanted
We're asking for You now

Put Your wisdom in our mouths,
Your life into our souls
Answer as we're crying out
Hear and make us whole

All we ever wanted,
You're all we ever wanted
And all we ever wanted
Is what we ask You for

All we ever wanted
You're all we ever wanted
And all we ever wanted
We're asking for You now

We focus on eternity
With wisdom love and grace
And with your hand upon our lives
We run this blessed race

All we ever wanted,
You're All we ever wanted
And All we ever wanted
Is what we ask You for

All we ever wanted
You're All we ever wanted
And All we ever wanted
We're asking for You now.

Saturday at the Soco Smoke Shop and Trading Post

Businessman,
Bonedigger,
Ghoul,
I shift my weight in the middle of nowhere,
9 to 5, till 9 on weekends,
I trade neon tomahawks,
Mock-beadwork keychains,
Plastic papooses,
To tourists.
I never let it slip that their Indian Country memories are made far
Away.
I never rebuke their cannibal ways.
I know what it takes for money, for power.
Even our dead are fodder.
As they board tour buses,
Clutching casino mugs,
Chicken plume headdresses,
Pawned powwow regalia,
Feeding on frybread,
Picking their dentures,
I wonder
How did I get here?
Did my life have an accident?
There's mercy in Thunderbird,
And that guy, Bud Wiser.
Or else, I might scalp Andrew Jackson,
Shoot into bingo with arrows drunk with blood,
Swallow seed beads by the handful,
Wrap my heart in feathers and leather,
Run and howl loud in pursuit of the moon.

A Eucharist of Sage

Here's what you do, you hand him the fork,
Shake hands with silver and trade him for tools.
Before the Chief makes you out to be some kind of fool,
Pick up your spoon and show him how to use it.

Chime fork tines against the rim of a plate,
Rounder and whiter than baked clay or baskets
And better for catching the runoff of grease,
Which you'll let him taste later, sometime after flour,
Then acquaint him with salt, white lard and fat meat.

Now, don't you neglect to give him the cup.
He'll need something to wash death down,
Carry oil to arteries, wither muscles, slow tongues
Which once out-rode, out-warred your guns.

Offer him Spirits in place of his soul,
So he'll agree to the exchange rate in Hell,
Fire for water, and ashes for dust,
He'll submit just to keep the drinks flowing.

Finally, finish and make you a country,
Built on the breaking of bread and bones.
Make bricks of pork and gates of foam,
Until eating begins to kill your own.

BLOOD MYTH

This ain't Neva-Neva Land.
Pixie dust can blind your eyes.
Try
Resist when the crocodiles lie.
That's no watch, just the sound of harm brewing.
No Tiger Lily here.
Only girls, named after stars,
Who crave lost boys who deal them like cards.
Who
Will never know what they got 'til it's gone.
Now,
Clap your hands.
Wish that away.

BEAUTIFUL WARRIORS

For all our Warriors, Troops and Veterans
U-wo-du-hi a-yi-s-ti-gi
We are on your side.
Do-hi-yi,
Peace,
Peace to you,
Peace to all who love you.
We are yours,
We are on your side,
Beautiful Warriors.
Breathgiver says yes,
You can rest
And your deeds will follow you,
Nv-ya ga-lv,
Honored stars,
In our songs.

VESSEL OF HONOR

"What is this game show?
How do they have so much to give away?"

I smile at my great-grandfather,
Squint through the famine of light in his farmhouse.
I give my voice a lilt,
The sun trying to explain itself to the moon.

I think he has help, Granddaddy.
His giveaway is courtesy of corporate competition.
Think of new cars as wild horses.

Granddaddy nods his head,
Spreading the scent of Vicks VapoRub and cedar
Between me and his TV.

We will pray, Grandma and I.
Granddaddy breathes through old ivory.
It is time for your marriage, for sons and for daughters.

You are such a fine girl, not lazy,
Not complaining like so many modern girls.
Your cornbread, your beadwork tell how you are.

You are such a good girl, not fast,
Not kissing or flirting like other women.
Your blood on your husband's sheets will reveal what you are.

Every day you wait is a sad day for us.
Every day you wait is one less warrior,
One less hunter,
One less Human Being in the world.

The gameshow bells count coup in the background.

Granddaddy's words ride bareback on the air.
Wait in smoke signals for me to tell him
That
Some Warriors now battle hand-to-hand with beer,
Water wed to Lysol or hairspray,
Charge away in one-eyed ponies to meet a broken end.

Some Hunters today stalk prey in Walmart,
Capture commodities from the BIA.
The bounty they snare is often illegal.
Fishing without asking can make the feds take offense.

It grieves me too much to tell him
That
From those who would be mothers,
Spirits have hidden the fathers.
So I whisper.

Granddaddy, it is this way.
Fewer people died from smallpox than from a lack of love.

It is quiet between us.
We know what is true.

THE WEIGHT OF SHIPRAH'S HEART

Moon and blood help me count days wisely,
Keep me counting as you come.
Legacy moans through my mouth,
Tastes my tongue.
Now you know what I need is you.

The meat of your hands gives me my reasons.
Your name is game in famine.
I sharpen my good arrow,
Feast on joy's fat and love's marrow.

I cry out from my blankets,
Wait and see,
Wait and see.
I have your heart,
And your harvest.

THREE KINGS

The whole world fits in your tiny hearts.
Your quickening explains
How these mountains touch Heaven.
You paint the first of the days after rain.
When floods make us despair of mud,
Your lives remind us of hours
Before the showers ended and we could see color
Beating, teasing the slant of the eye
Into running at the drumming of ceremony songs.

HAGAR'S HYMN

We have done what we should not have done.
We have known what we should not have known.
We have not used wisdom when we should.
We have not done all we could.

Skwa-ti-ni-se-sti yi-ho-wa e-lo-ti ga-i-suh-i
Ni-go-hi-luh ni-go-hi-luh ski-ste-li-ske-ste-yo-go.

We have owned what we should leave alone.
We have left our lands for other homes.
We have called no other name but Yours.
We have asked for what is ours.

Sgi-sde-li sgi-sde-sgi-li-sgi to-hi de-sgi-sa sta-ni.
Ni-go-hi-luh ni-go-hi-luh do-da-guh-no-gi-sta-ni.

THE SONG OF DEBORAH

Sing us songs about blood,
Hymns about blood quantum.
Wail round dance songs with moaning refrains,
In waves,
Of transfusions and graphic designs
Bloodroot in sewers
Now confined
In tubes
Transfused
From
Merciful donors hoping for halos,
Pirates draining plasma for grand entry and change,
A range
Of singers
Crossing blood
As we dance
From mixed
To diluted
To saved.

STRIKE THE GROUND

Historical Trauma Problems, but our hearts are pure,
Sure,
Surer than blood shot, colonialism's cure.

We aim our good arrows,
Always hit marrow,
Rife
With strife,
We stop the knife of genocide.

SERPENT OF BRASS

"Merry Christmas," rasps the pawnshop clerk,
"Buy a candle or a knife?"
Someone sliced a hole in his throat,
His atonement for the smoke he loved.
I give him the ticket, nine months old.
It floated to me while I bathed in the river.
So I crossed the border to find out what was left.
What would I leave here?
What would make money during the storms of a life?
A sign in the case states in sprawling hand,
"Indian Fingerbones+arrowheads—genuine."
What a difference a boundary makes.
"Are those fingers from now or then?" I inquire.
"Couldn't tell you, Princess," coughs the clerk.
"That's the reason we call it DEAD pawn."
He cackles, smoke seeps through seared fissures.
He grins like he was clean once,
But I know he never was.

I leave that ticket on his counter.
I fear it drips blood.
I run towards home until I hear drums.

THE SACRAMENT OF BARBECUE
For all our Troops and Veterans

Ask Cousin Bill why he went to war?
Hear him answer, so he could return and desire again
What once he loved.

Don't stare at Silas.
Else he'll snap that he didn't lose his legs,
He gave them.

"Buddy gave me an atlas one Decoration Day," Nathaniel says,
Points with his lips, the NDN way.
"The way to Canada is lined in yellow,
Iraq, Old Babylon, outlined in blood.
Keep to the Underground Railroad,
He warned,
Called the fires in the desert points to avoid."
Nathaniel went twice anyways.

Pass the potato salad to Lee, who says, "if they call you for battle,
Call on me.
I'll take your place in foreign lands.
All I ask
Is your firstborn, boy or girl, name them Lee,
Teach them how I went, bound, to keep America free."

THE BOOK OF DANIEL

None of this could I have known,
As I harvest an heir,
From seed richly sown,
Quickened and watered by blood and hormones.

Called to life by time and fire,
And mercies of Heaven,
Not idols, desires,
Made manifest as Creator says "yes."

INCIDENT AT ECHOTA (I TOOK A DNA TEST ON THE AIR AND THIS IS WHAT IT SAID)

My mother made a multicolored girl,
From the days of the week,
In the arms of my father.
The angel on duty threw up his hands.
"You cannot expect me to guard such a girl,
Not when you pay me in cedar and blankets."

Creator kept him assigned to his post.

Now I am grown, still colorful,
Less girl.
I give my angel no trouble.
He sits and reads at night,
Approves of all my beadwork,
Admires all my poetry.

We go fishing on Fridays,
My singing is the bait.
He stirs starlight and red flowers
To give me life without regrets.
When they tell I am all the colors,
We both know this is Grace.

LIFEGIVERS

This is a story of roses,
Imposes
That line in the sand that somehow is drawn,
In fidelity,
In loyalty,
In love.

This is a song of forever and then some,
None left standing,
All blown away,
By verses,
By flow,
By meter.

A heart steadfast with beats and rhymes,
A mind that mines the streets,
For songs that shine.

The Remarkably High Price of Forgiveness on the Prairie
For my Sister, Robin

The man who says he loves her
Leaves her
Shattered
Battered
Heart shards in a jar of what once she loved

Another who says he loves her
Does the same
A game with
No name
Spirit care far from where once she loved

Yet God who says He loves her
Never leaves her alone
On her own
Salves her soul full of scars to map how she loved

Souls who know we love her
Ask and answer
Problems solved
Evolve
Her life is loved

CAPTIVITY TURNED

Death rubs long legs together,
A violin signaling famine,
Sawing the air with chitin and lard,
Promising lack in minor keys,
Preaching hunger while gnawing plenty.
A thick, black cloud, every insect for himself,
A wise man sees trouble and hides himself
In damp cellars of sorrow and pantries of grief.
The simple goes on and is destroyed
By loss and reservations in sharp succession
Until every man does what is right in his own eyes,
Which is almost, always, achingly wrong.
While the locusts laugh,
We fold our hands and eat our own flesh.
Enemies of death,
Wait for singers who know redemption's song.

QUIVER FULL

Poets owe no debt to sleep.
Before you wed one, you should have known this.
Now you're surprised by the songs of starlight
Long before daybreak, as dreams meet spirit.

The measure of rest is a cruel transaction.

I understand and soothe you,
But God has things to do.
Chronicle our lives, our tribes, by starlight,
Streaming through windows, across the page
Of the prophecies I keep by the bed,
For such a time as this.

Poets often rhyme in shadows,
Our fingers writing lines that seem straight.
Daystar shows them crooked as sticks in water.

I compose by candles we waxed last summer,
Useless in any dark but this.
Constellations teach us to number our days.

On the nights when I must prophesy,
Every moonbeam matters.
All the verbs are impressed into service.
Those seasons, those times,
We light fires.

You roll over,
Anointed to love through meter.

HERALD ANGELS

Go-hi i-go-hi
At the present day

o-gi-na-li-i o-tsa-tla-nv-dlv-i
my friends, we are all sisters and brothers

tsu-da-lenvda got-lv-hisodi
things get better

a-le ga-lie-liga.
and I am glad.

a-da-deyodi
instruct

de-deyodi
teach

os-dv galo-his-di.
a good way.

Hi-da-li-he-li-ga
Let us all be happy

Hi-tsa-li-he-li-ga
You all be happy

Ha-li-he-li-ga
You be happy

Ga-li-e-li-ga
Let me be happy

Hi-na-li-he-li-ga.
You and I be happy.

Ha-li-he-liga, a-da-ge-y(u)-dihu-do-da-gwi-sv-i.
Be happy,
love all day long.

ONE JUDGE
For Daniel

In the night seasons, the Oceans cry,
Stars collide, we know it's your time.
In the night seasons, the Prophets dance
Raise their hands, see visions in trance.

In the night seasons, the Warriors chant,
Moon retreats, streams light in a slant,
In the night seasons, the Hunters come
Haunt hollers and rivers and wait for the sun.

Come morning, we all speak in tongues.

THE SEED OF THE KING
For Daniel

Dream in sweetgrass,
In sage,
In Stars.

Dream cedar in baskets, woven and scarred
With crimson dye and bloodroot lines.

Dream of Red Paint and how we sing,
How you were conceived a holy thing,
When seas and tigers combined in our veins,
Poured stains of rain into Stomp Dance flames
And birthed your heart in the desire of fire.

Dreams of panthers mean you too,
How Creator found us wanting you,
Above all men,
To win

Our land, our love, our lives.

CANOE JOURNEY
For Daniel

Ancestors go down to the sea in ships,
Seeking sea glass shards of hearts,
Settled in streams of starlight and gold,
Navigating by maps etched deep in the soul.

Descendants row canoes under the sun,
Count the waves until there are none,
Arriving at plenty when the voyage is done,
Realize home is wherever life has begun.

Legacies dance by the light of the moon
The haka, the hula, the fire dance, too.
As they finish, they give us you,
The destination of all our journeys.

BLOOD MOON

Blood in the Moon.
This is a song about signs and wonders.
Ponder the last note of the last Stomp song
That lingers in our blood,
Pounds on and on
In our hearts, our souls, our Tribes.
Earth and Fire.
This is a song about pirates and liars.
Question the strange song in our own land
That takes the fat right from our hands.
March on and on
In a Trail of Tears.
Pillars of Smoke.
This is a song about a knife in a treaty
Watch soldiers and missionaries show themselves greedy.
Sing on and on
In other tongues.
Wonders in the Heavens.
This is a song about Generation Seven.
Stomp Dance, Sundance, all unleavened
Dance on and on
Victory won.

Magnificat

The taste of sea salt reminds me of you.
The sound of Green Corn songs does, too.
Smell of sweet grass, wet after rain,
Came
As you each were given your names.
Thunder and Lightning intertwined in a chain,
Moon and Morningstar enmeshed in flame
Of an eternal fire.

BIOGRAPHY

Dawn Karima is a two-time Global Music Award Winner. This Silver Arrow Award Winner won a Native American Music Award for her CD, *The Desire of Nations* and was nominated for an Indigenous Music Award for her CD *The Stars of Heaven*. This Indigenous Artist Activist Award Winner is the author of two novels: *The Way We Make Sense*, a Finalist for the Native American First Book Award, and *The Marriage of Saints*, a volume of University of Oklahoma's American Indian Studies Series and a Finalist for the New Mexico Book Award. This Rare Life Award Nominee is also the author of *What to Do if You Don't Know What to Do* and the Co-author of *Children Learn What they Read*, a book about multiculturalism in children's literature. This Women of Essence Global Award Winner hosts *A Conversation with Dawn Karima*, an award-winning, internationally syndicated radio show and podcast. A graduate of Harvard University, she holds an MFA in Creative Writing from The Ohio State University and a Ph.D. conducted at University of Kentucky/Trinity Seminary.

North Carolina's Qualla Boundary Reservation is home to this Josie Music Award Nominee and Spread Love Award Winner. A prominent speaker, educator, artist and consultant, she is available to hire for speaking engagements, presentations, media making, academic instruction and spiritual inspiration.

Dawn Karima, also known as "Mother of Nations," loves her life as a Mother, most of all.

COLOPHON

Titles for *Mother of Nations* are set in Lucida Sans. Designed by Kris Holmes and Charles Bigelow in 1993, the font is designed to support the most commonly used characters defined in digital typography.

The body text itself is set in Garamond. It is a serif typeface, named for sixteenth-century Parisian engraver Claude Garamond.